D1495272

CONTENTS

Pages 2 and 3, (*Corydoras leucomelas*) by MP & C. Piednoir; Pages 34 and 35: (Cardinal tetras, *Paracheirodon axelrodi*) Photo by H.-J. Richter

longtail gold danio
chinese algae eater

©1996
By T.F.H.
Publications,
Inc., Neptune,
NJ
07753 USA

•
T.F.H.
Publications,
The Spinney,
Parklands,
Denmead,
Portsmouth
PO77AR
England

Your First
TROPICAL FISH

—— **Dr. Herbert R. Axelrod** ——

YF-116

Livebearers

Among the most highly recognized and sought after aquarium fishes are those in the group known as *livebearers*. The *livebearers* are fishes that deliver their young alive, not in the usual egg form. The newborn fishes are completely formed and free-swimming at birth. There are several reasons that the livebearers are so desirable. For starters, they exhibit magnificent coloration, are commonly available, are relatively inexpensive, and for the most part are easy to care for and breed.

Guppy (*Poecilia reticulata*)

Heading the list for a combination of beauty and popularity among the livebearers is the Guppy. Guppies have been bred in almost every conceivable color pattern and fin shape. Unlike the wild-caught strains from South America, which are comparatively dull in coloration, commercially bred Guppies offer an endless display of lustrous colors and long flowing fins. It's therefore no surprise that the Guppy's general popularity doesn't end with the beginning hobbyist, but continues also among serious aquarists and international Guppy organizations.

Caring for and breeding the Guppy in the beginner's aquarium is relatively simple. A standard aquarium in the 10- to 20-gallon range is more than sufficient. Guppies will thrive in the home aquarium with proper aeration and filtration. Providing suitable water requirements is not at all difficult. Moderately hard water with a pH that is slightly alkaline works best. An aquarium heated between 76 and 78°F is also strongly recommended. These conditions also apply to the other livebearing species that are covered here.

Preparation of breeding quarters for the Guppy requires minimal work. Most pairs will spawn under normal aquarium circumstances. For better results raise the temperature of the tank a few degrees. This will often speed up the initial spawning process.

The normal gestation period of the female Guppy and the other livebearing species covered in this book is between 4 and 6 weeks. A carefully selected pair of Guppies that are about three or four months old are usually mature enough for breeding. The newly born fry may range in number anywhere between 20 and 100. Unfortunately, the mortality rate of the young Guppy is high. The Guppy's cannibalistic

The Guppy, *Poecilia reticulata*, has been selectively bred to produce a wide selection of phenomenal colors and unique fin shapes. Most beginners choose the Guppy as their very first tropical fish when setting up their aquarium. Photo by A. Noznov.

instinct is quite common among livebearers. Therefore, an aquarium supplied with fine-leaved plants should provide numerous hiding places and shelter for the recently born baby fish. After birth the young active Guppies are free-swimming, with ravenous appetites. There are several over-the-counter fry foods that provide adequate nutrition, but the addition of some live foods such as microworms or baby brine shrimp ensures optimal growth and health. Guppies that have reached maturity will readily accept a variety of foods, both prepared and frozen, but are especially fond of live foods.

If the main objective is to produce offspring, Guppies should be kept in tanks by themselves. Otherwise, the Guppy makes for an excellent community fish when housed with small non-aggressive tankmates such as tetras or other livebearers. It's safe to say that more people have learned how to care for tropical fishes by starting with the Guppy than with any other fish. There is a wide tolerance and flexibility enjoyed when dealing with the Guppy, so it's no wonder the Guppy makes for a superb beginners' fish.

Swordtail (*Xiphophorus helleri*)

The Swordtail, originally from southern Mexico and vicinity, is another colorful livebearer that is easy to maintain and breed. Overall, they basically require similar care as the Guppy. In today's aquarium hobby there are several interesting varieties to choose from. Some of the more easily attainable strains that are usually heavily stocked and sold in the retail market include the Red, Green, Black, Marigold and Tuxedo Swordtails. Other varieties of the Swordtail include the regular Lyretail and Hi-Fin Lyretail Sword. *Xiphophorus helleri* inherited its common name from the male's sword-like extension of the caudal fin.

The Swordtail's peaceful temperament makes it an ideal beginners' fish. Aggression is rare, although bullying by Swordtails of both sexes is far from unknown. Sexing and breeding the Swordtail can be achieved successfully with relatively little trouble even for the novice. The female Swordtail is capable of giving birth to as many as 150 young at one time. The fry are easily raised and cared for. Feeding the Swordtail entails little difficulty. They will accept all regular aquarium foods including flake, frozen and live foods.

Although wild specimens of the Swordtail may exceed 5 inches in length, captive-bred individuals will rarely reach 3 inches. Their wonderful coloration more than makes up for their limited size.

Platies are among the most popular livebearers for the home aquarium. Numerous color strains have been developed by breeders such as this beautiful gold "Salt & Pepper" Platy. Photo by Dr. H. Grier.

Platies (*Xiphophorus* species)

When a hobbyist makes mention of the Swordtail its relative, the Platy, is usually not far behind in recognition and merit. The Platy is another excellent livebearer that strongly deserves the popularity it often receives. It provides brilliant coloration to any aquarium. It's a peaceful and active fish that will almost never show any signs of aggression.

Platies come in a wide selection of color varieties including solids and combination colors, with the red platy being the most commonly seen in the hobby. They are reliable breeders capable of producing broods of young at a rate of once a month. The typical Platy may produce well over 100 fry (baby fish), but 60 to 80 is more common.

Feeding Platies is similar to both the Swordtail and Guppy.

Mollies (*Poecilia* species)

Although the various Molly species should not be technically considered easy to maintain beginners' fish, they remain extremely popular with new hobbyists, and therefore will be covered on that basis alone. In general most livebearers prefer some salt added to their water. Mollies require a substantial amount of salt content in their water. A teaspoon of salt to every gallon of water is sufficient and will make keeping them a lot easier.

Mollies are rather peaceful and are capable of living with most other aquarium occupants that are able to tolerate their water specifics. Hard alkaline water that is between 74 and 78°F is ideal. Aquarium lighting should be provided between eight and ten hours daily along with a well planted aquarium. Although most dry and frozen foods will be taken, additional greens in the diet are absolutely necessary. Mollies require lots of vegetation, first for food and second to protect the young if a pair are bred and young fish are expected.

The Molly is frequently bred in the home aquarium. A pregnant female Molly's body gradually swells prior to giving birth. Given a well planted aquarium, most Molly parents will not eat their young, which makes raising the fry more convenient. Different types of Mollies often seen in the hobby include the Marble, Lyretail, Balloon Body, and the popular Sailfin (*Poecilia latipinna*). The Sailfin is a rather attractive species, but is also one of the most abused aquarium fish in the respect that few hobbyists make an honest effort to learn about their living specifics. Sailfins are not ideal community fish and prefer to be left alone in a warm aquarium with large amounts of vegetation.

A large school of Cardinal Tetras,*Paracheirodon axelrodi,* offers a brilliant display of color to any aquarium. Tanks that are decorated with dark backgrounds and gravel will enhance the beauty of these truly remarkable fish. Photo by MP &. C. Piednoir.

Egglayers

There are many more different types of egglaying species than livebearing species. Some fishes lay adhesive eggs which stick to plants, and some lay non-adhesive eggs which fall to the bottom of the aquarium. *Egglayers* are broken down into groups that correspond roughly to the fishes' taxonomic families. There are many factors that determine the incubation period of eggs. Depending on the type of species being bred, water temperature, lighting, and general water specifics, eggs may hatch at different rates and intervals.

TETRAS

The popular group of egglaying fishes that are almost always seen in the home aquarium are the characins (tetras). These pleasant, small, schooling fishes make wonderful additions to the hobbyist's tank mainly because several species can be mixed in limited aquarium space.

Neon Tetra (*Paracheirodon innesi*)

The Neon Tetra (*Paracheirodon innesi*) is a beautiful fish with an intense fluorescent blue stripe, and with red and white throughout the body. It's very peaceful and an attractive asset to any community aquarium. They are similar to other tetras in that their intense coloration becomes more dominant when kept in a school of a dozen or more. The Neon will accept most flake and frozen foods and especially prefers an occasional treat of live brine shrimp or daphnia. One vital consideration when choosing these fish is that they will often become the dinner of a larger species capable of swallowing them. Any fish that appears large enough for such a threat should be avoided in the Neon aquarium.

Neons are very difficult to spawn and beginners are not very successful. Only advanced aquarists are successful in breeding the Neon Tetra. Neons available for purchase in the aquarium hobby often are imported rather than commercially bred.

Cardinal Tetra (*Paracheirodon axelrodi*)

Easily confused with the Neon Tetra for a number of reasons is the Cardinal Tetra (*Paracheirodon axelrodi*). With only minor differences in coloration the Cardinal Tetra and Neon Tetra are almost exactly alike. The difference is that the Cardinal has more red

Spawning the Flame Tetra, *Hyphessobrycon flammeus*, is not difficult and even the beginner is often successful. Not only is the Flame Tetra easy to breed, but it is also very peaceful, hardy and colorful, which makes it ideal for the community aquarium. Photo by H. J. Richter.

and more blue coloration and grows slightly larger. The Cardinal, like the Neon, will tolerate several tank companions and is an excellent community fish. An aquarium with minimal lighting and soft slightly acidic water works best. Decorative plants of both the live and artificial varieties are sufficient.

The Cardinal is not a fussy eater and will accept flake, frozen and live foods. A heated aquarium balanced between 70 and 75°F is perfect. Cardinals are similar to the other schooling tetras in that a minimum of six of them should be placed in the aquarium. Breeding the Cardinal is not a simple task. Most breeding attempts by the beginner are unsuccessful.

If the beginning hobbyist is searching for that extra boost in aquarium color, both the Neon and Cardinal Tetra are fantastic choices especially when placed in a dark graveled tank or situated in front of a black background.

Flame Tetra
(*Hyphessobrycon flammeus*)
The Flame Tetra (*Hyphessobrycon flammeus*) is a very beautiful and peaceful fish from Rio de Janeiro in South America. They are incredibly active and are not at all shy, and actually prefer being out in the open in small schools exhibiting themselves. Suitable water conditions can

be provided in no time at all. The Flame Tetra prefers slightly acidic water with temperatures between 75 and 78°F. A combination of flake, frozen, and live foods of various types are always eagerly accepted. A balanced diet ensures maximum growth, which is rarely over 2 inches in length with this species. Spawning the Flame Tetra is strongly recommended for any curious hobbyist. It's easily accomplished and the rewards of creating your first newly born fish are delightful. Spawning will take place on any fine-leaved plants provided by the hobbyist. Two plants that are popular choices are *Myriophylum* and *Cabomba*. Several eggs are released by the female and hatching occurs in two to three days. Once the fry begin to swim they may be fed finely chopped foods or infusoria. Shortly after, the aquarist will be raising his or her new Flame Tetras to maturity, which is usually 6 to 8 months.

Head-and-Tail Light Tetra
(*Hemigrammus ocellifer*)
Head-and-Tail Light Tetras (*Hemigrammus ocellifer*), widely distributed throughout the Amazon region, are very tranquil and hardy fish. Head-and-Tail Lights are easy to sex as the males have longer and more slender bodies and a unique streak which runs across their anal fin. In the

Zebra Danios, *Brachydanio rerio*, are among the easiest egglayers to care for and breed. A clean, well aerated aquarium that is sufficiently heated is all that is needed to successfully keep these attractive schooling fish. Here a pair (male in front of egg-laden female) engage in spawning maneuvers. Photo by H.-J. Richter.

aquarium they prefer temperatures between 76 and 78°F. The pH requirements are somewhat flexible and a neutral reading of 7.0 is adequate. Although almost all types of flake foods are taken, an additional feeding of frozen and live foods are more beneficial.

In order to fully appreciate the reason this tetra received its common name, a fluorescent light used on top of the aquarium will show off their gleaming spots located on top of the eye and at the base of their tails. Breeding the Head-and-Tail-Light is not difficult as long as an aquarium in the 10- to 20- gallon size is provided. Once a healthy mature pair are selected there are very little additional aquarium preparations needed.

Bloodfins (*Aphyocharax anisitsi*)

Bloodfins (*Aphyocharax anisitsi*) have been in the aquarium hobby for many years and continue to hold their own as far as popularity is concerned. It's no surprise since they make ideal community fish and require minimal tank maintenance. These small schooling fish will flourish in a clean, well-aerated aquarium that is heated to around 76°F. Bloodfins are somewhat flexible as far as water temperature, but their brilliant red coloration will show up better in a warm, well lit tank. Bloodfins will quickly dart about the aquarium in search for food. They are not picky eaters and almost all commercially prepared foods are accepted.

Breeding the Bloodfin can be achieved with little difficulty but does require some preparation. A standard ten gallon aquarium will suffice, and some marbles placed on the aquarium bottom are helpful. Since the eggs of the Bloodfin will not stick to plants or the aquarium glass, they can safely fall on the marble bedding provided. The pair can then be removed and the small eggs will hatch in 30 to 36 hours.

Glowlight Tetra (*Hemigrammus erythrozonus*)

A popular egglayer from Guyana is the peaceful Glowlight Tetra (*Hemigrammus erythrozonus*). This is another tetra species that can't be fully appreciated unless displayed under correct aquarium lighting. A dark, decorated aquarium that is well planted will usually do the trick. It's safe to say that the Glowlight Tetra is one of the most peaceful of all the many tetras in today's aquarium hobby. Their water requirements include soft water with a slightly acidic pH, heated between 74 and 78°F. Glowlights like many of the tetras are active swimmers and will occasionally jump out of the water.

The White Cloud, *Tanichthys albonubes*, is extremely flexible when it comes to both the amount of aquarium space needed and provision of suitable water conditions. White Clouds make excellent additions to the community aquarium and are strongly recommended for the new hobbyist. Photo by H.-J. Richter.

Therefore, a covered aquarium is strongly recommended to discourage such antics.

Dry foods are commonly accepted, but supplements which include varieties of frozen and live foods such as brine shrimp are preferred. Aquarium water temperatures raised to around 80°F or slightly above will usually trigger spawning after 24 hours. During the spawning process semi-adhesive eggs are laid on the thick bunches of plants that the hobbyist provides. Most fry will hatch within three days and will eagerly eat live foods.

CYPRINIDS (Family Cyprinidae)

Most of the cyprinids fall into the category of "egg-scatterer" as far as spawning is concerned. In simple terms these species of fishes have no preference as to where their eggs are laid. Cyprinids scatter their eggs and let them lie where they fall.

Zebra Danio (*Brachydanio rerio*)

Although small in number of species the genus *Brachydanio* includes two popular fishes that work well in the community aquarium. The Zebra Danio (*Brachydanio rerio*) is probably the most popular egglaying fish. A community aquarium that's clean and well aerated is usually all that is needed in successfully keeping these fish. This small,

active schooling fish accepts almost all types of aquarium foods. Breeding is also very simplistic and requires minimal preparation. A heated aquarium set at about 75°F is sufficient. A breeding pair of Zebras will scatter non-adhesive eggs in either thick bunches of plants or over marbles. There are several other breeding methods, but for the most part they have the same purpose — to keep the parents from eating their young.

Leopard Danio (*Brachydanio frankei*)

The Leopard Danio (*Brachydanio frankei*) is another respected *Brachydanio*. Leopard Danios have attractive colors, are easily bred, and are incredibly active in the aquarium. A standard aquarium that is aerated and filtered provides excellent living quarters for these fish. The Leopard Danio will spawn in similar fashion to the Zebra. After spawning is complete there may be as many as 1,000 eggs! Live, frozen, and dried foods are willingly taken. The Leopard Danio fry are easily raised on newly hatched live brine shrimp. Since both the Leopard Danio and Zebra Danio offer such flexibility in housing and care, they make ideal beginners' fishes.

White Cloud (*Tanichthys albonubes*)

One of the most flexible and

The Albino Tiger Barb is one of the many forms of *Capoeta tetrazona*. With the exception of the occasional chasing and harassing of other tankmates they make excellent beginners' fish. A popular method for conquering their habitual pestering of other fishes is to house at least half a dozen individuals in an aquarium. Photo by Dr. H. Grier.

easy to care for of all aquarium fishes are the White Clouds. From a technical standpoint they're not really tropical fish. They actually prefer a cool aquarium, but are capable of living in warmer water temperatures if need be. A water temperature anywhere between 65 and 85°F is tolerable. The White Cloud has a pleasant disposition and works well in most community tanks. A school of White Clouds can easily adapt to a small aquarium in the 5- to 10-gallon range. They may be fed all types of flake foods along with varieties of frozen and live foods.

The White Cloud has the reputation of being one of the easiest aquarium fish to spawn. Male and females can be kept together in a heavily planted aquarium. They should be conditioned on a diet that consists of live foods and shortly thereafter will spawn and produce fry. The White Cloud fry can be easily confused with the fry of Cardinals or Neons because of their great similarity in color. The fry may be fed newly hatched brine shrimp until they're old enough to eat other popular fish foods.

Tiger Barb (*Capoeta tetrazona*)

Another group of cyprinids that are commonly kept in the hobby are the fishes referred to as barbs. The most desirable is the Tiger Barb (*Capoeta tetrazona*). Despite Tiger Barbs' feisty antics, they remain a hobby favorite greatly attributable to their wonderful coloration and easy breeding habits. The only drawback is that the Tiger Barb is inclined to nip the fins of its tankmates. In most cases long-finned fishes are usually the unfortunate victims. The most popular remedy for conquering their occasional aggressiveness involves placing at least a half a dozen to a tank. This scenario will usually result in the fish playfully harassing each other rather than other fishes in the tank.

Several varieties have been developed from the original standard Tiger Barb. Among these are the Albino, Blue, and Moss-Green. Spawning is the same for all the varieties. An aquarium equipped with plenty of vegetation and a carefully selected pair will usually do the trick. Water preferences include soft, slightly acidic water with a temperature anywhere between 70 and 85°F. Aquarium temperatures between 83 and 85°F are recommended for breeding purposes. Young fish that are fed infusoria and newly hatched brine shrimp will grow rapidly if provided with adequate aquarium space. Full-grown specimens may reach over three inches in length. Adult Tiger Barbs can be fed a variety of foods including flake, frozen, and

Although not brilliantly colored, the Checker Barb, *Capoeta oligolepis*, makes an ideal addition to any aquarium. They are small, peaceful, easily bred, widely available and inexpensive. Photo by H.-J. Richter.

live food. Additional greens in the diet will also enhance the adult fish's coloration and overall health. Generally speaking, Tiger Barbs may be considered favorable community fish if they're kept away from long-finned varieties such as Bettas and Angelfish.

Cherry Barb (*Capoeta titteya*)

The Cherry Barb (*Capoeta titteya*) is a lovely colorful little barb that ranks high as far as popularity goes in the eyes of the aquarist. It's a peaceful and undemanding fish that requires little preparation in setting up suitable living requirements. Its brilliant red color is intensified during breeding and can be maintained if the fish is kept under ideal conditions. Cherry Barbs prefer a well planted tank with a pH that is slightly acidic (6.6 - 6.8). A heated aquarium stabilized between 76 and 78°F is preferred. Almost all types of aquarium foods are accepted including flake, frozen, and live foods.

A pair of Cherry Barbs that have had sufficient time acclimating to each other can spawn without much difficulty. Eggs will often be scattered among fine-leaved plants or over the gravel bed. There may be as many as 200 young. Fry will usually hatch between 24 to 36 hours and the parents should be removed immediately since they will often eat their young. The Cherry Barb is a pleasant barb and is an exceptional addition to any beginner's aquarium.

Checker Barb (*Capoeta oligolepis*)

The Checker Barb (*Capoeta oligolepis*) is not gloriously colored but has a lot to offer to the aquarium hobby. It's small, hardy, peaceful, easy to breed, and is strongly recommended for the community tank. Water composition is not critical and a slightly acid pH and temperature between 74 and 76°F are ideal. Besides taking almost all aquarium foods available, the Checker Barb will occasionally eat lettuce or spinach as a special delicacy. They have a special preference for greens in their diet and to observe them eating aquarium algae is not uncommon.

Distinguishing the sexes of the Checker Barb is easy. The male is darker with a bright red-orange tinge and black markings. Both the male and female have extremely large attractive scales in comparison to their overall size. The Checker Barb is easy to spawn and the newly born fry are extremely small thus requiring very small foods.

ANABANTOIDS

These types of fishes are also known as labyrinthfishes. These unique fishes have a special respiratory organ that enables them to extract oxygen from the

The male Siamese Fighting Fish, *Betta splendens*, is one of the most beautiful and popular of all labyrinthfishes. Bettas are often displayed in small tanks, but aquariums of greater size are more beneficial in achieving optimum growth and health of the fish. Photo by K. Tanaka.

air. There are several species that make excellent community tank occupants. Many anabantoids build bubblenests at the aquarium surface and are extremely popular in the hobby. The male anabantoid in most cases builds the nest and will single-handedly guard the young.

Betta (*Betta splendens*)

One of the most widely recognized anabantoids is the beautiful Betta or Siamese Fighting Fish (*Betta splendens*). The brilliant colors and long fancy finnage of the male Betta have made it an aquarium delight for both the beginner and advanced hobbyist. Its ability to swim to the aquarium surface and take in air makes keeping the Betta in tiny tanks possible. This is often the case in most aquarium shops where male Bettas are displayed in small aquariums usually less than a gallon in capacity. The Betta should be housed in a larger tank to allow for more swimming space and less of a chance for aquarium pollutants to quickly build.

The male Betta is much more attractive in comparison to the female. The male's long flowing fins are available in a variety of colors including blue, red, green, and a creamish yellow as well as combinations thereof. The females have short fins and are less colorful. Two male Bettas can't be kept together. If placed in the same aquarium they will fight intensely until one dies. In the community aquarium they may be placed with both livebearers and tetras. The Betta is a slow swimming fish and should not be placed with some of the more active barbs.

A well heated aquarium between 78 and 80°F is most suitable for the Betta. A variety of foods are accepted including flake, frozen and live brine shrimp, bloodworms, and daphnia. Breeding the Betta can be achieved with great success. The male begins the spawning process by building a bubblenest at the aquarium surface. Once the eggs are released from the female the male will take them in his mouth and store them in the nest. Tank water that is raised a few degrees will usually cause the eggs to hatch in two to three days. Betta fry may be fed infusoria, newly hatched brine shrimp, and whiteworms.

Dwarf Gourami (*Colisa lalia*)

The Dwarf Gourami (*Colisa lalia*) is a hardy fish that adjusts extremely well to aquarium life. They have peaceful dispositions and will rarely show any signs of aggression. The breeding habits of Dwarf Gouramis are very similar to the other bubblenest builders with one exception. The Dwarf will include a very deep substantial bubblenest consisting of vegetation, twigs, and other

The male Flame Gourami, a color variety of *Colisa lalia*, is extremely colorful and very popular with the beginning hobbyist. Dwarf Gouramis will rarely exceed two inches in length, which makes keeping them in the standard aquarium more convenient. Photo by Dr. H. Grier.

debris. In the aquarium the Dwarf Gourami will flourish in a neutral pH and should be provided with adequate amounts of natural sunlight. Water temperatures in the high 70's are most preferred. Dwarfs are not fussy eaters and alternating live food with both frozen and dry foods is helpful.

The male Dwarf Gourami offers marvelous color with its brilliant red irregular transverse stripes with streaks of blue. The females are more golden with fewer stripes. As you may suspect the Dwarf Gourami will not grow large in the aquarium and rarely exceeds two inches in length.

Pearl Gourami (*Trichogaster leeri*)

The Pearl Gourami (*Trichogaster leeri*) is one of the most highly praised of all the Gouramis. Its splendorous coloration combined with their less than imperative aquarium needs has made them a well respected fish. Water conditions are not critical. A heated aquarium around 76°F is ideal. An aquarium that is roomy and well planted caters to their somewhat shy personalities. A dark gravel bed and floating plants are also helpful. The Pearl Gouramis have such small mouths that large pieces of food should be avoided and small dry and live foods may be fed exclusively.

The Pearl Gourami will spawn in the community aquarium, but a separate breeding tank is desirable. The size of the bubblenest and the number of eggs are both large. A thousand eggs are not uncommon. During spawning, the Pearl Gourami doesn't indulge in aggressive behavior that is sometimes typical of other related species. Once the eggs are laid, the female may be removed as the male will tend to the nest. As soon as the eggs hatch the male should also be removed. The fry should be fed infusoria or very fine foods.

Blue Gourami (*Trichogaster trichopterus*)

Another popular Gourami species is the Blue Gourami (*Trichogaster trichopterus*). There is also a golden color variation of the Blue Gourami which goes under the common name of Gold Gourami. Blue Gouramis are the same as Gold Gouramis with the only exception being the color. A large well heated aquarium supplied with plenty of vegetation ensures the best opportunity for a pair to spawn. For the most part Blue Gouramis will make decent community fish if not housed with fishes that are too small. A good spawning temperature is around 77°F, with a slightly acid pH.

Feeding the Blue Gourami is not a problem. They willingly

Angelfish, *Pterophyllum scalare*, are one of the most popular aquarium fishes of all time. The Golden Marble Angel is only one of the many different strains of angels that make superb community fish. Photo by K. L. Chew (Gan Aquarium Fish Farm).

accept most foods whether they be dried, frozen, or live. The Blue Gourami is capable of growing rather large in the aquarium and may very well exceed six inches in length. Therefore, as mentioned earlier, any small tankmates should be avoided to prevent them from being swallowed or harassed.

Kissing Gourami (*Helostoma temminicki*)

The Kissing Gourami (*Helostoma temminicki*) is a very difficult fish to induce to spawn. Their difficult breeding habits haven't taken away from their widespread popularity in the home aquarium. Kissing Gouramis' large protruding lips will occasionally lock together. This unique embracing action is where their common name derives from. Researchers that have studied these fish have concluded that this action is some type of threatening behavior display. From a more practical standpoint their lips are used to press against ornaments, plants, or the glass sides of the aquarium in order to suck off slime or algae that covers them. The Kissing Gourami will grow extremely large in the aquarium and therefore should be provided with large enough living quarters. For the most part they make reasonably good community fish when kept with species of their own size.

The Kissing Gourami will prosper when housed in a hobbyist's tank with hard water and a neutral pH. An aquarium heated to around 76°F is suitable. Several floating plants can provide shade. The Kissing Gourami is a timid fish that dislikes a brightly lit tank. It's a ravenous eater that requires enormous amounts of food which usually consists of brine shrimp, bloodworms, and varieties of greens. Aquariums rich in algae are beneficial in catering to their vegetarian eating habits. If algae is unavailable, lettuce and spinach make suitable substitutes. When all else fails regular basic flake food is almost never turned down.

CICHLIDS

When a beginning aquarium hobbyist hears the term cichlid the word that immediately comes to mind is trouble. Over the years the cichlids have acquired a bad reputation among amateurs because they've been known to dig up the aquarium, damage plants, and fight among themselves and other species. Contrary to popular belief most of these problems can be solved by simply setting up suitable living quarters and learning more about their natural habitat and general needs. Therefore, I won't come to a hasty conclusion and simply dismiss them as unsuitable for the first aquarium, but will describe some species

The Albino Oscar, *Astronotus ocellatus*, is the most recently developed variety of this very popular cichlid. Oscars have ravenous appetites and will certainly swallow any tankmates small enough to fit in their mouths. Photo by Dr. H. Grier.

that are popular nonetheless and often kept successfully in the hobby.

Angelfish (*Pterophyllum scalare*)

Angelfish (*Pterophyllum scalare*) are recognized by every aquarist worldwide. It's probably one of the most popular egglaying fishes ever known. Millions upon millions of tank raised fishes are commonly sold all over the world. There are several varieties of Angelfish that have been produced through hybridizing and fixed inbreeding. The Angelfish is suitable for the community tank as long as its other inhabitants are also of the quiet and peaceful variety. The Angelfish has extremely long dorsal, anal, and pelvic fins that many fast swimming fin-nipper fishes find most appetizing.

A clean, heated aquarium that has a temperature of around 75°F and a pH that is neutral or slightly acidic is most appropriate. Angelfish may be fed most freeze-dried or live foods. They also have a special preference for daphnia. A spacious tank provided with ribbon-leafed plants and the right water specifics provides an ideal aquarium for spawning. Some other modern breeding methods include using empty tanks with no substrate. A piece of slate or acrylic placed on an angle provides a spawning surface for the breeding pair. In other circumstances Angelfish ignore all the spawning surfaces offered and deposit eggs on filter or heater tubes. Breeding pairs can be recognized from their tendency to pair off and can later be transferred to a special tank laid out as recommended above. Both parents will care for the eggs and the fry will usually hatch after three days. The parents will take great care of their young as they gather them in tight schools at the bottom. Later, the fry must be fed fine foods in the form of infusoria and newly hatched brine shrimp.

Jack Dempsey (*Cichlasoma octofasciatum*)

The Jack Dempsey (*Cichlasoma octofasciatum*) is very popular with the beginning hobbyist who has a fancy for any of the larger cichlids. They have incredibly bright light blue spots which are more noticeable on the males in comparison to the females. The Jack Dempsey's tankmates must consist of fish that are of comparable size, for any smaller fishes are certain to be bullied. If you're looking for a peaceful, placid fish, the Dempsey is certainly not your best alternative.

A large, well decorated aquarium with plenty of rocks and driftwood is strongly recommended. This allows for plenty of hiding places and enough area for the Dempseys

Melanochromis auratus is one of the most commonly kept African cichlids. The Auratus is extremely territorial and must be provided with numerous caves and rock structures. Photo by M. Gilroy.

to establish their own territories. Aquarium water averaging around 76°F is best. The Jack Dempsey has a hearty appetite like most of the larger cichlids. Pelleted cichlid food, beef heart, brine shrimp, and both tubifex and bloodworms are taken.

Spawning the Jack Dempsey is not difficult. Most eggs will be laid on stones or pieces of wood that have been thoroughly cleaned by the parents. A thousand wriggling fry are not at all uncommon and they will grow very rapidly if raised on daphnia, tubifex, and other finer foods.

Oscar (*Astronotus ocellatus*)

The Oscar (*Astronotus ocellatus*) is one of the most popular of the larger cichlids. Perhaps it's the special bond that aquarists often develop between the fish and themselves. Oscars appear to have a more intelligent and friendly attitude than most other fishes. More likely it's their constant search for food that makes them appear so intent on following the owner's every move outside of the tank. The Oscar is like the Dempsey and must be kept with larger cichlids that are similar in size. Smaller, defenseless tankmates will be harassed and, in a more common scenario, swallowed.

A spacious tank with a deep sandy bottom provided with rock, wood, and caves will satisfy the Oscar's habitat needs. They will often be seen habitually digging on the bottom of the aquarium leaving most plants uprooted. The Oscar is a voracious fish and will eat almost anything including beef heart, dried food, and any live food, such as small fishes and insects.

Some of the basic types of Oscars often available include the Red, Tiger, Black, and the newest remarkable strain, the Albino.

Blue Zebra (*Pseudotropheus zebra*)

African cichlids are becoming more and more popular with the hobbyist. Some aquarists feel that their intense coloration greatly resembles some of the fancy saltwater fish. The Blue Zebra is certainly one of the most popular of the African cichlids. It offers a lot of color and can be successfully kept in the home aquarium. The Blue Zebra doesn't grow extremely large in the hobbyist's tank but can be still considered a bully for its size.

This species is very territorial and should be supplied with a well decorated aquarium. A large aquarium allows for adequate swimming space and plenty of room for the establishment of individual territories. An aquarium heated to around 78°F is ideal. The Blue Zebra is omnivorous and requires a balanced diet of both animal and vegetable matter. A wide

Corydoras aeneus is just one of many popular corys available that make excellent community tank occupants. The bronze or green corys shown here are the easiest to find and care for. Photo by Dr. H. J. Franke.

selection of aquarium foods are taken including bloodworms, tubifex worms, beef heart, and various vegetable substances such as algae, spinach, or lettuce. Basic aquarium flake foods are also readily accepted.

Pseudotropheus zebra and most other cichlids from Africa's Rift Lakes like tanks that are heavily decorated with rocks that they can hide among.

The Blue Zebra is a type of cichlid called a mouthbrooder. Mouthbrooders carry their eggs and young in their mouths. The newborn fry use the mouths of their parents as refuge until they are capable of surviving on their own. The fry may be raised on fine live foods such as baby brine shrimp.

Auratus (*Melanochromis auratus*)

Another common African cichlid is *Melanochromis auratus*, commonly called Auratus. An aquarium with hard, alkaline water with a water temperature between 76 and 80°F works best. The Auratus is a very territorial and aggressive fish that requires a large aquarium. Bigger tanks with well-secured rock structures provide adequate retreats for the Auratus. The Auratus, like the Blue Zebra, is a mouthbrooder and is easily bred by the beginner.

Auratus will accept all standard aquarium foods including frozen, freeze dried,

and live food. Additional feedings of vegetable matter such as algae, lettuce, and spinach are also taken.

CATFISHES

Most beginners' tanks are incomplete without some type of catfish. There are many different families of catfishes available for the home aquarium.

Corydoras species

The most widely recognized species of catfishes belong to the genus *Corydoras*. These small and peaceful catfishes are not only commonly available, but are easily maintained in the home aquarium. The corys have the remarkable ability of swallowing air from the aquarium surface and absorbing its oxygen through the intestinal lining. In the aquarium they may rest peacefully on the gravel and without further warning will race to the aquarium surface for a gulp of air. Corys that make numerous trips to the aquarium surface may be the first signs that the water quality has begun deteriorating.

Corys may be kept with varieties of tetras and livebearers. A school of at least six corys is best since they have a tendency to be uneasy and shy if kept alone. A standard aquarium that is well filtered, aerated, and stocked with live plants will support most of the corys' needs. Special attention should also be given to the type of aquarium gravel used. Sharp-edged gravel can cause damage to the corys' barbels. A slightly acidic pH with a heated aquarium set at 76°F is ideal. Of the several varieties of corys that are available some of the more common types are the Bronze, Skunk, and Peppered. The corys will eagerly accept all types of flake, frozen, and live foods. They also have a special preference for live bloodworms or tubificid worms.

Corys have an unusual method of group spawning. Three males to every female should be placed in the chosen breeding tank. Sexing the corys can be done with a great deal of accuracy. Females are generally bigger and broader than the males. Lowering the water temperature between 5-7°F will usually trigger spawning. Depending on the species of cory being bred, eggs may be deposited on plants or flat rocks, but most often on the sides of the tank glass. There may be as many as 700 eggs and when hatched the fry will accept microworms or baby brine shrimp.

Suckermouth Catfishes (*Hypostomus*)

Suckermouth catfishes (various genera) are often sold under the common name "plecostomus" or just plain "algae eater." Most are seen relatively small when being sold in aquarium shops, but may reach nearly a foot in length when full grown. Their claim to fame in the hobby is definitely not their overwhelming attractiveness, but likely is based on the fact that they do an excellent job of cleaning the algae that will often grow on aquarium glass, plants, and rocks. Not only do they demand heavy amounts of vegetable matter in their diet, but they will also feast on live or frozen bloodworms and tubifex worms. However, it should be emphasized that without vegetable matter as the main source of diet the suckermouth catfish will not survive long.

Suitable water conditions include an alkaline pH (7.1-7.4), and an aquarium heated to between 75 and 80°F. Most suckermouth cats will become active at night following their nocturnal instincts. There have been very little if any reports of *Hypostomus* successfully breeding in the home aquarium. For the most part small suckermouth cats make perfect community fishes and will rarely show signs of aggression with the exception of an occasional dispute among themselves. On the other hand, larger suckermouth catfishes may become aggressive toward smaller tankmates and may even be seen sucking the protective slime coating off other fishes.